Everything

For
Everyone

ENDING POVERTY THROUGH
CREATIVE VISUALIZATION

ELEANOR McMANN

Bestselling author of
THE UNIVERSE IS YOU

PUBLISHED BY INVISIBLE HAND PRESS
C/O THE GREAT DIVIDE MOVIE LLC
HTTPS://THEGREATDIVIDEMOVIE.ORG/

ISBN 979-8-89342-156-9

Baby Food for the Mind

An introduction by Bill Dates

Founder of Macrohard Systems

When I first met the ravishing Eleanor McMann – back before I single-handedly invented the internet, cured every disease known to man, conquered death, got more ass than a toilet seat, built a time machine to remake history in my own image, kickboxed Musk, Zuck, and Bezos into comas, and commandeered the nanobot hordes to intergalactic glory – money was tight, and so was I.

That night, in fact, I was drunker than a dozen Gulianis. But I knew the McMann clan's untold trillions could buy a private island for every sex offender on Earth. With that kind of scratch, I could get Macrohard in seconds.

So when I finally managed to corner her out back, flashing my intellectual property at her, she just gave me a winsome grin and said, "That's adorable, honey. *But what's in it for me?*"

At that very moment, it all became clear. My internet would be one of supreme self-gratification, wherein the needs of all would appear to be instantly met. In the process, it would open a bottomless hunger for more. And I would dangle the universe as bait.

Who could resist? And why the hell would they?

This is the message of Eleanor McMann. Want more. Demand more. Glorify the moreness until it is the allness. And put yourself in the glowing center, until every bit of it surrounds you, flows toward you endlessly. Like baby food for the mind. Or beets out of a baby's backside.

And though Eleanor wouldn't invest a goddam dime in the enterprise, I think we all owe her an enormous debt of gratitude. (A notion with which I'm quite sure she will agree.)

With *Everything for Everyone*, she is offering us her heart. Or maybe her soul. Or whatever the fuck passes for her mind, at any given moment.

But mostly, her spirit is the spirit of the internet itself. Voracious. Insatiable. Like a mirror with teeth.

Why would you even want to resist it?

So please, enjoy Eleanor's timeless words. Every time you buy her bullshit, I get a whooooole lot richer. And I'm already richer than God.

Sincerely,
Bill "The Boner" Baits

Money is not real. Only you are real.

When problems seem too hard,

imagine that they're very soft.

Hug your problems until they love you.

1+1=2. Win + Win = Success

All life is beautiful, no matter how difficult.

Let yourself be beautiful.

There is an amazing sunset every day

whether or not you can see it.

You contain both failure and success.

When you believe in yourself,

only success can get out.

Your mind is not in the world,

the world is in your mind.

Visualize all the money you need.

Now visualize more.

You will always need more.

There is no social contract

until you draft one yourself.

Your desires are not born.

You are born through your desires.

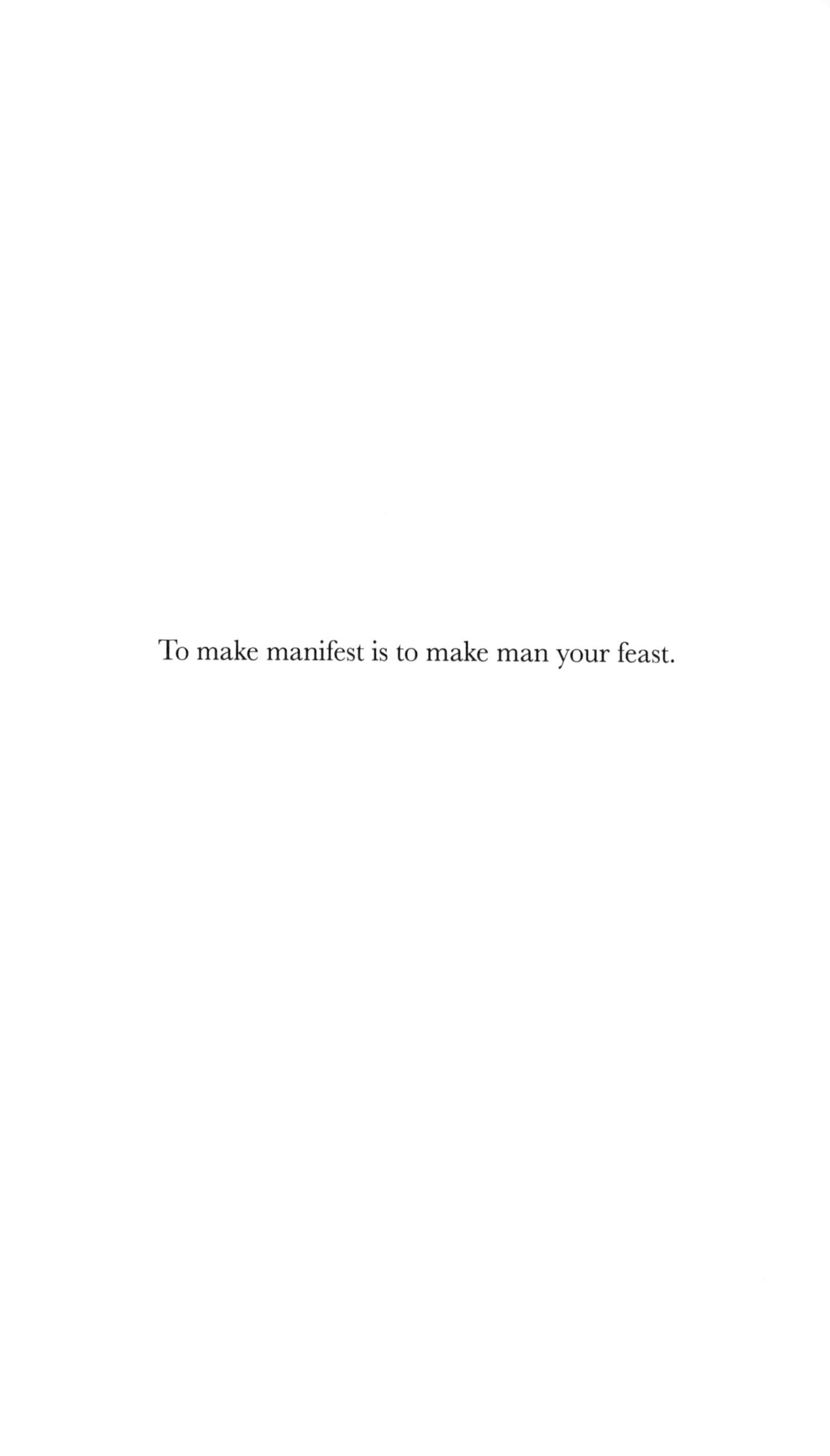

To make manifest is to make man your feast.

Everybody wants to be number one.

But what they should really want is to be ONE.

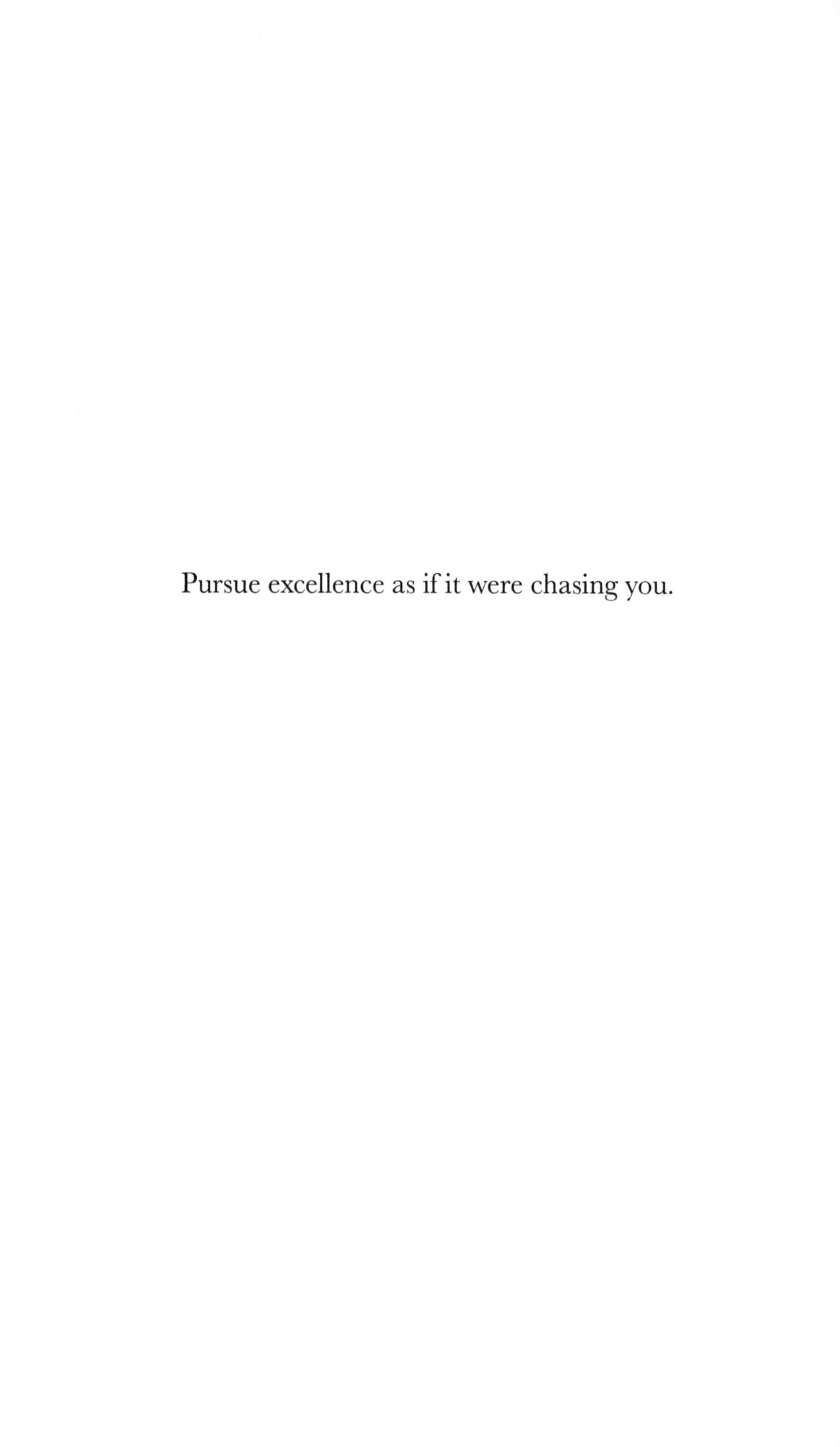

Pursue excellence as if it were chasing you.

The root of being is both seeing and freeing.

Catch the waves of desire

because they will lead to the sea of fulfillment.

The first taste is a step

into knowing the whole meal.

When you make mastery your mistress,

you become a mystery to the masses.

Go with the flow.

No,

the other flow.

The triumph of compassion

is that you know how I feel.

When the weather is profoundly uncomfortable,

it means you need to be more comfortably profound.

I am never more alone

than when no one will listen to me.

When I trust my own wisdom,

I know that I'm right.

The forest of ideas is yours for the taming.

If the world is your oyster,

and you don't like oyster,

order the lobster

or maybe surf n' turf.

Tend to your orchard

or your fruit will be rotten.

The most beautiful thing I ever saw…

was me.

If it tastes bad,

spit it out from your energy field.

When people discover the glory of the universe,

you should always say "thank you."

Pearls are made from irritation.

What could be made from celebration?

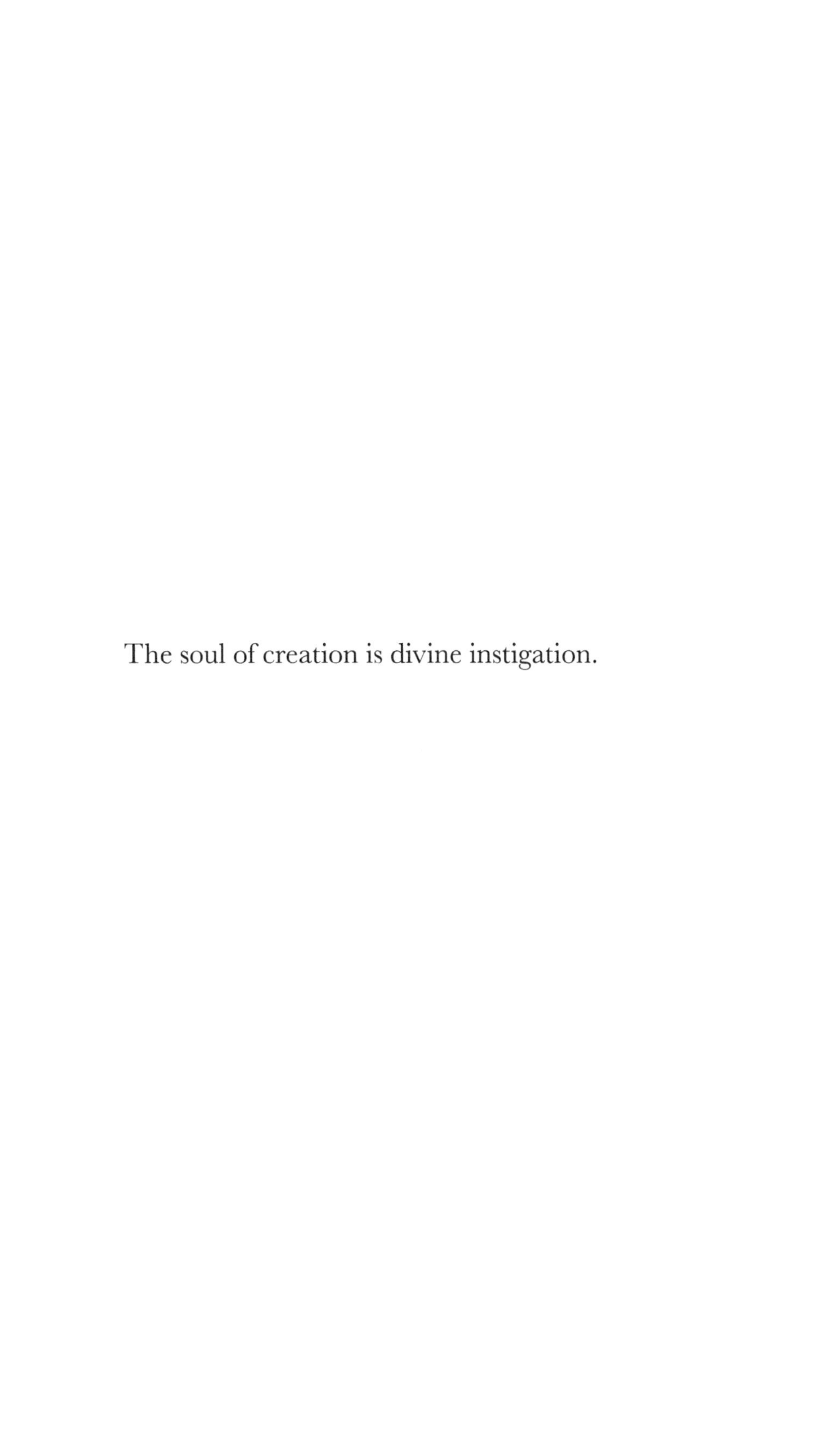

The soul of creation is divine instigation.

The first spark makes a holy fire.

If you ignite me, I'll show you the way.

My electric vehicle is love.

Paradox means that you just don't get it.

True understanding comes

when you realize I was right.

When you ask a lot of questions,

you're not in the know.

Why walk on water,

when you can walk in the air?

If you can see me,

I can see you better.

I know you are.

But what am I?

Self is you in me.

True freedom

is

somebody else's expense account.

Don't let the music of the spheres

drown out your inner harmony.

Manifest now, or you will miss the how.

Meditation

is the deep tissue massage of the soul,

and the gods are really hot,

and you dropped your towel.

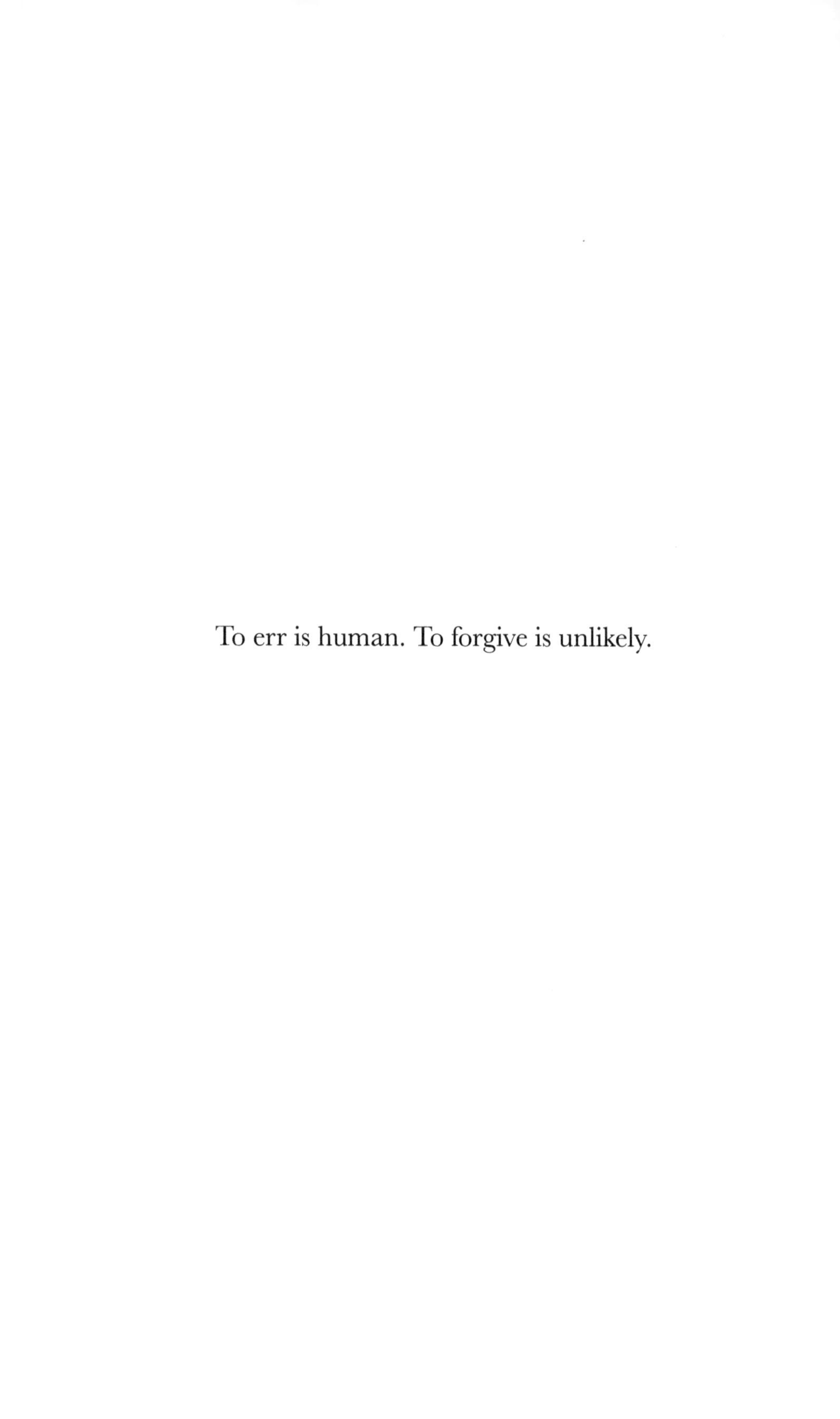

To err is human. To forgive is unlikely.

Why think of Barbie and Ken

when the world is your Zen?

Never underestimate the power of self importance.

If you want to be free,

just ask me!

When everyone around you is in doubt,

cash in.

Greed is just abundance misunderstood.

There is more than enough for everyone.

Just remember the line starts here.

My satisfaction is everybody's business.

And they all have a part to play.

Have you ever marveled

at the beauty of a flower?

Me too.

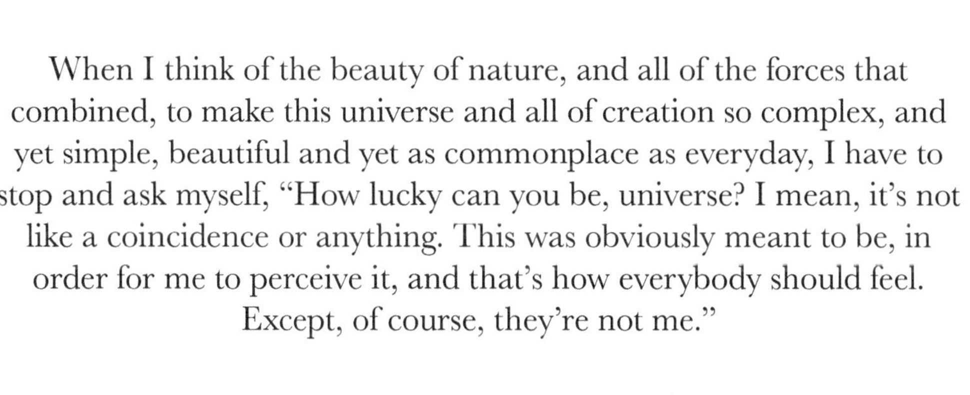

When I think of the beauty of nature, and all of the forces that combined, to make this universe and all of creation so complex, and yet simple, beautiful and yet as commonplace as everyday, I have to stop and ask myself, "How lucky can you be, universe? I mean, it's not like a coincidence or anything. This was obviously meant to be, in order for me to perceive it, and that's how everybody should feel. Except, of course, they're not me."

The magnitude of your obsession

magnifies your soul possession.

Jibber jabber means flibber flabber.

True being is to offer at the altar of me.

To make a world free of suffering,

you cannot believe in the suffering of others.

Blah blah blah blah blah blah blah blah blah blah blah blah blah blah blah blah blah blah blah blah Blah blah blah blah blah blah blah blah blah blah blah blah blah blah blah blah blah blah blah Blah blah blah blah blah blah blah blah blah blah blah blah blah blah blah blah blah blah blah blah Blah blah blah blah blah blah blah blah blah blah blah blah blah blah blah blah blah blah me me me me me me me me me me me me me me me me me me me me me me me me me me me me me me me me me me me me me me me me me me me me me me me me me mme me me me me me me me me me me me me me me me me me me me me me me me me me me me me me me me me me me me me me me me me me me me me me me me me me me me me me me mme me me me me me me me me me blah blah blah blah Blah blah blah blah blah blah blah blah blah blah blah blah blah blah blah blah blah blah blah blah Blah blah blah blah blah blah blah blah blah blah blah blah blah blah blah blah blah blah blah blah blah blah Blah blah blah blah blah blah blah blah blah blah blah blah blah blah blah blah blah blah Blah blah blah blah blah blah blah blah blah blah blah blah blah blah blah blah blah blah blah blah Blah blah blah blah blah blah blah blah blah blah blah blah blah blah blah blah blah blah blah blah blah Blah blah blah blah blah blah blah blah blah blah blah blah blah blah blah Blah blah blah blah blah blah blah blah blah blah blah blah blah blah blah blah blah blah blah blah me me me me me me me me me me me me me me me me me me me me me me me me me me me me me me me me me me me me me me me me me me me me me me me me me me me me me mme me me me me me me me me me me me me me me me me me me me me me me me me me me me me me me me me me me me me me me me me me me me me me me me me me me me me me mme me me me me me me me me me me me me me me me me me me me me me me me me me me me me me me me me me me me me me me me me me me me me me me me me me me me me me me me me me me me me me me me me mme me me me me me me me me me me me me me me blah blah blah blah blah blah Blah blah blah blah blah blah blah blah blah blah blah blah blah blah blah blah blah blah blah Blah blah blah blah blah blah blah blah blah blah blah blah blah blah blah blah blah blah blah blah

blah Blah blah blah blah blah blah blah blah blah blah blah blah blah blah blah blah blah blah blah blah blah Blah blah blah blah blah blah blah blah blah blah blah blah blah blah blah blah blah blah blah Blah blah blah blah blah blah blah blah blahmeme me me me me me me me me me me me me me me me me me me me me me me me me me me me me me me me me me me me me me me me me me me me me me me me me me me me me me me mme me me me me me me me me me me me me me me me me me me me me me me me me me me me me me me me me me me me me me me me me me me me me me me me me me me me me me me me me me me me me me me me me me me mme me me me me me me me me me me me me me me me me me me me me me me me me me me me me me me me me me me me me me me me me me me me me me me me me me me me me me me me me me me me me me me me me me me me me me me me me me me me me me me me me me me me me me me me mme me me me me me me me me me me me me me me me me me me me me me me me me me
me me me me

mememememememememememememememememememememememememememememem
emememememememememememememememememememememememememememememe
mememememememememememememememememememememememememememememem
emememememememememememememememememememememememememememememe
mem

mememememememememememememememememememememememememememememem
emememememememememememememememememememememememememememememe
memememememememememememememememeeeeeeeeeeeeeeeeeeeeeeeeeeeee
eeeeeeeeeeeeeeeeeeeeeeeeeeeeeeeeeeeeeeeeeeeeeeeeeeeeeeeeeeee
eeeeeeeeeeeeeeeeeeeeeeeeeeeeeeeeeeeeeeeeeeeeeeeeeeeeeeeeeeee
eeeeeeeeeeeeeeeeeeeeeeeeeeeeeeeeeeeeeeeeeeeeeeeeeeeeeeeeeeee
eeeeeeeeeeeeeeeeeeeeeeeeeeeeeeeeeeeeeeeeeeeeeeeeeeeeeeeeeeee
eeeeeeeeeeeeeeeeeeeeeeeeeeeeeeeeeeeeeeeeeeeeeeeeeeeeeeeeeeee
eeeeeeeeeeeeeeeeeeeeeeeeeeeeeeeeeeeeeeeeeeeee

The 39 Steps
TO MAXIMUM POTENTIAL

STEP # 1

Believe in yourself.

STEP # 2

No, actually, believe in me.

STEP # 3

Don't listen to them. They're crazy.

STEP # 4

Do you think I'm lying to you? Are you serious?

STEP # 5

Because I could totally leave right now.

STEP # 6

Hey! Nobody talks to ME like that!

STEP # 7

Don't you know who I am?

STEP # 8

That's it. I'm calling Security.

STEP # 9

Oh, so now you want to be nice?

STEP # 10

Show me.

STEP # 11

Show me the money.

STEP # 12

Show me how nice you are.

STEP # 13

That's it. Now get down on your knees.

STEP # 14

That's right, you little worm. Crawl!

STEP # 15

Make good soil.

STEP # 16

In your undies.

STEP # 17

Oh, you like that, don't you?

STEP # 18

You disgust me.

STEP # 19

Come here.

STEP # 20

Are you deaf? I said COME HERE!

STEP # 21

Okay, that's better.

STEP # 22

Come to Eleanor. That's right, baby.

STEP # 23

You're such a tool.

STEP # 24

A beautiful tool.

STEP # 25

More precious because you're mine.

STEP # 26

And you will always worship me.

STEP # 27

Always and forever.

STEP # 28

There is no turning back.

STEP # 29

Because you're nothing without me.

STEP # 30

Okay, I'm bored now.

STEP # 31

Stop crying, god damn you.

STEP # 32

Security?

STEP # 33

Yes, I think I heard someone at the back door.

I'm so... I'm so scared.

Yes, please hurry.

And bring a gun.

Maybe several.

STEP # 34

You hear that, you pathetic little rabbit turd?

STEP # 35

You'd BETTER run!

STEP # 36

Run! Run! Ha ha ha ha ha!

STEP # 37

Thank you, officer.

You're just in time.

STEP # 38

Would you like to get comfortable?

STEP # 39

Believe in me.